I0191141

THE NEW COVENANT'S POWER

Douglas R. Behm

THE NEW COVENANT'S POWER

Copyright © 1983 by
The C.S.S. Publishing Company, Inc.
Lima, Ohio

All rights reserved. No portion of this book may be reproduced or utilized in any form or by any means, electronic or mechanical including photocopying, without permission in writing from the publisher. Inquiries should be addressed to: The C.S.S. Publishing Company, Inc., 628 South Main Street, Lima, Ohio 45804.

Permission is given to reproduce those portions of the service needed for congregational participation.

All Scripture quotations are from the Revised Standard Version of the Holy Bible.

1/87 2.T

1412/ISBN 0-89536-600-2   PRINTED IN U.S.A.

TABLE OF CONTENTS

Preface V

MAUNDY THURSDAY
  Christ's Power for New Community................ 1

GOOD FRIDAY
  Christ's Power for New Compassion.............. 11

EASTER SUNDAY (Sunrise)
  Christ's Power for New Celebration............. 20

PREFACE

This booklet contains a variety of services and suggestions, which may be used together or separately, for Maundy Thursday, Good Friday, and Easter Sunrise. These three major historical occasions for Christian worship are unified under the theme, "The New Covenant's Power." In our Lord Jesus Christ we now live under a new agreement (covenant) with our one true God.

Maundy Thursday, with an historical emphasis on the Lord's Supper, as well as Christ's commandment for his disciples to love one another, brings into focus "Christ's Power for New Community." On this occasion Word and Sacrament heal our broken relationships with God and others and establish the possibility of new community in Christ.

Good Friday, with an historical emphasis on the actual events of the crucifixion, as well as our atonement through Christ's suffering, death, and resurrection, gives us opportunity to receive "Christ's Power for New Compassion," which he still offers all people. With Calvary, the atoning work of Christ is "finished," leaving our world the possibility of receiving new love in the forgiveness of God.

Easter Sunrise, with an historical emphasis on the overwhelming joy of Christ's triumph over sin, death, and the power of the devil, captures "Christ's Power for New Celebration." Never before this Easter Day has the world had such Good News to celebrate. Even today there is no greater power in heaven or earth than the power to see "what no eye has seen, nor ear heard . . ." (1 Corinthians 2:9) as we have "The New Covenant's Power."

Maundy Thursday

Christ's Power for New Covenant Community

Background

Maundy (or Holy) Thursday provides a special occasion for us to focus on the power of Christ's new covenant — through his words and deeds — for creating new life among his disciples. As this new covenant life grows in us, through recalling the power of Christ's new commandment of love, through witnessing the example of Jesus' own deeds of love, and through sharing the living presence of his love in Holy Communion, we experience *Christ's power for new covenant community.* Therefore, on this special day we recall, experience, and share anew the depths and extremes of Jesus' love, that we might follow *together* in the footsteps of his intentional lifestyle as we become his new creation.

Setting

1. This service could be a traditional sanctuary service with Holy Communion.

2. This service could be a service of Holy Communion set in an appropriate fellowship room with tables and chairs for the congregation ("Table Communion.")*

3. "Table Communion" could be held as an early service with a traditional service at a later time.*

*Note: The purpose of "Table Communion" is *not* to re-enact a seder meal or Passover but to provide a less formal motif in which fellowship might be experienced with eye contact and conversation as groups gather around tables for the Lord's Supper. Of course, "Table Communion" could appropriately follow or precede a congregational supper or meal.

Symbols

1. A towel could be used, perhaps draped over one shoulder of the minister, during all or part of the service.**

2. A section of paper towel could be handed to every person as they enter or leave the service, or as the sermon is being presented at Table Communion, as a symbol of our new covenant community of love and service.**

3. As the service begins, or during the sermon, the minister could actually wash the feet of other prepared persons, taking an appropriately placed towel for use.**

4. A pitcher and basin, along with a towel or roll of paper towels, could be prominently placed on a front table (or such a picture on an easel).

5. For "Table Communion," goblets might be provided for each table, with the wine being poured from a single wine bottle on the head or main table at the proper time.

6. Bread could be broken from common loaves of leavened or unleavened bread.

7. Participants could administer communion elements to one another.

**Note: In using a towel, Jesus provided us with an image which we constantly use in our daily lives. Because we do not have hot sand or always wear sandals, it is difficult to recapture the necessity and importance of the soothing foot washing of Jesus' culture. Instead, we might do well to use this towel image to make a memorable connection between such an everyday, ordinary symbol in every household and such extraordinary cleansing (renewing) love. Our goal might be to use a towel, an item which we contact constantly in our daily living (yet in a different way than in Jesus' culture) to remind us daily that we live in the New Covenant community of faith and forgiveness, love and service.

Congregational Introduction of the Maundy Thursday Service
(for written or oral presentation prior to service beginning)

"THE NEW COVENANT'S POWER" is our focus this Holy Week and Easter as we hear once again the Good News (Gospel) for our life together in Jesus Christ. On Maundy (or Holy) Thursday, we have set aside a special time to remember that *Our Lord's New Covenant Power Creates a*

New Community! Today (Tonight), along with all his Church, *we recall* the power of Jesus' new commandment, "love one another; even as I have loved you." (John 13:34) *We witness* the power of our Lord's own love in action. *We share* the power of his redeeming presence in Holy Communion.

(FOR TABLE COMMUNION ADD:) By gathering in a setting of tables, we intend to capture something of the intimate community fellowship of the upper room. As we share Christ together in this hour of love, we also experience the possibility of the new covenant community established by Jesus many years ago.

(A statement of local beliefs and/or practices concerning Holy Communion may follow.)

THE MAUNDY THURSDAY SERVICE
The New Covenant's Power:
Christ's Power for New Community

The Gathering of New Community People

THE PRELUDE

THE HYMN (stand)
A hymn should be chosen for both content and familiarity. Images could include: God's love for us, the Church as God's community for us, and/or love for others as the characteristic of God's community. One of the following might be used (if not in your hymnal, be sure you have copyright permission to reproduce):
Where Charity and Love Prevail
Love Consecrates the Humblest Act
What Wondrous Love Is This
The Church's One Foundation
They'll Know We Are Christians by Our Love

THE INVOCATION (L-Leader; C-Congregation)
L: We are God's people, chosen for life in his new covenant community.
C: *We are God's people, responding to the wonderful deeds of our Lord Jesus Christ.*
L: We are God's people, chosen for life in his new testament Church.

4

C: *We are God's people, living individually as members of his whole body.*

L: In Christ we are God's new creation.

C: *We welcome the changes the Lord has made.*

L: "Our competence is from God,

C: *"Who has made us competent to be ministers of a new covenant."*

L: "All this is from God, who through Christ reconciled us to himself;

C: *"For our sake he made him to be sin who knew no sin, so that we might become the righteousness of God."*

L: In the name of the Father, and of the Son, and of the Holy Spirit,

C: *We gather as God's new covenant community by the power of our Lord Jesus Christ.*

L: (A Maundy Thursday Prayer of the Day or Collect)

C: *Amen.*

(Scripture references and quotes above are to the following: 1 Peter 2:9; 1 Corinthians 12:27; 2 Corinthians 3:5b-6a; 2 Corinthians 5:17-18)

The Source of New Community Beliefs

THE FIRST LESSON (sit): Jeremiah 31:31-34

THE PSALM (sit): Psalm 116 (or Psalm 116:10-17)

THE SECOND LESSON (sit): 1 Corinthians 11:23-26
(A well-prepared reading of the First Letter of John may be substituted for the lessons above or may be used as another option for the Proclamation below. The Gospel reading should not be omitted for any reason.)

THE HYMN and/or ANTHEM
Suggested hymns include;
Now We Join in Celebration
O Savior, Precious Savior
Let Us Break Bread Together
O Bread of Life From Heaven
Lord Speak to Us, That We May Speak
Today Your Mercy Calls Us
Jesus Sinners Will Receive

The anthem should suggest Christ's actions as being the basis of our new creation, our new life, etc. Care is required to keep the individual believer connected to the new community of disciples in the words of the anthem or hymn.

THE GOSPEL LESSON (stand): John 13:1-35

THE PROCLAMATION (sit):

Option 1: A traditional sermon might be presented based on the Gospel and the actions of Jesus as he gives shape to the creation of his new covenant community of disciples. We have the power (1) of Jesus' direction (or commandment); (2) of Jesus' example (or serving); (3) of Jesus' cleansing (or forgiveness).

Option 2: A proclamation might center around the Hymn, "Love Divine, All Loves Excelling." A reflection on stanza one, then sing stanza one, etc.; or present sermon with thoughts of all stanzas, concluding sermon with full hymn.

Option 3: Laity or youth might alternately read short quotations from various portions in the Scriptures concerning our life together as disciples of the new covenant community. When appropriate, such verses could be prepared on 3 x 5 cards and given to worshipers as they enter to read at this time. A mature Education Committee or adult class might be involved in researching such verses. (Care should be used to keep the emphasis on our Lord's action of love in creating his Church, rather than just on our actions of response.)

Option 4: A well-prepared dramatic reading of 1 John.

THE HYMN (sit or stand)
Love Divine, All Loves Excelling

The Confession of New Community Faith

Option 1: Apostles' or Nicene Creed
Option 2: Recite Ephesians 2:4-10, facing one another.
Option 3: Recite 1 Corinthians 13 together.

The Response of New Community Love

6

Sharing Our Gifts and God's Blessings (Offerings)

OFFERING

OFFERTORY RESPONSE
In Christ There Is No East or West
Blest Be the Tie That Binds
Take My Life, That I May Be
We Give Thee But Thine Own
Praise God, From Whom All Blessings Flow (Doxology)

Sharing Our Sins and God's Forgiveness
(Confession; sit or kneel)

L: It is the power of our Lord Jesus Christ which opens our eyes to our sins and our hearts to his forgiveness, for "there is no disctinction, since all have sinned and fall short of the glory of God, they are justified by his grace as a gift, through the redemption which is in Christ Jesus." (Romans 3:21b-24)

C: *"If we say we have no sin, we deceive ourselves, and the truth is not in us. If we confess our sins, he is faithful and just, and will forgive our sins and cleanse us from all unrighteousness. (1 John 1:8-9)*

L: I am the Lord your God. You shall have no other gods.

C: *Forgive us, Lord, for our failure to always love and trust you above all else. Create new values in us, and direct us in arranging our daily priorities according to your will in Jesus Christ.*

L: You shall not take the name of the Lord your God in vain.

C: *Forgive us, Lord, for the ways we misuse and abuse your name, as well as the many times we forget about you completely. Help us to receive and honor Christ's new covenant with us by increasing prayer, praise and thanksgiving.*

L: Remember the Sabbath day, to keep it holy.

C: *Forgive us, Lord, for the times we fail to seek and search your Word for the way, the truth, and the life we need. Turn us anew toward Christ and his new community of faith as we respond to your Spirit's promptings.*

L: Honor your father and your mother.

C: *Forgive us, Lord, for living our lives according to our* own opinions and conveniences and forsaking family and friends. Help us to submit ourselves to the way of Christ in our relationships with others.

L: You shall not kill.

C: *Forgive us, Lord, for the times we live only for ourselves, neglecting the needs of our community and environment. Transform us to be ambassadors of your love in all the world and caretakers of your earth.*

L: You shall not commit adultery.

C: *Forgive us, Lord, for the abuses we make of your highest and best creation in our thoughts, words, and deeds. Help us to see your image in every person that we might fulfill your purposes in all our lives.*

L: You shall not steal.

C: *Forgive us, Lord, for the ways in which we seek to justify our own selfish desires and greed by making dishonest statements, half truths, or generalizations about others. Help us to be honest and upright so that we can be your servants as you build up your kingdom through us.*

L: You shall not bear false witness.

C: *Forgive us Lord, for our unkind, unloving, and prejudiced words which only serve to defile us who speak them and tear apart your community. Empower us to hold our tongues, unless we speak words in kindness, even about our enemies.*

L: You shall not covet.

C: *Forgive us, Lord, for our pretenses before you in trying to live by the way of the world instead of the cross and self-denial. Empower us so to follow you in all our relationships that we might be called the people of God, disciples of Christ.*

L: (Absolution/Forgiveness Pronouncement) (Leader stands at altar while people continue kneeling or sitting.)

Option 1: A traditional absolution may be exchanged between the leader and congregation.

Option 2: A statement of individual forgiveness may be spoken to each person desiring to come forward to a central place. The verse from Ephesians 2:8 might be used as the minister places a hand on the person: "For by grace you have been saved through faith; and this is not your own doing, it is the gift of God."

Option 3: A statement of forgiveness may be spoken to each person as the leader moves among the people and places a hand on each person at a "Table Communion" setting. The verse from 1 John 1:7 might be used: "We walk in the light, as he (God) is in the light, we have fellowship with one another, and the blood of Jesus his Son cleanses us from all sin."

Sharing Our Needs and God's Name (Intercessions; stand)

Option 1: The people may present petitions individually, according to their concerns, with an appropriate response from the leader and/or congregation following each petition.

Option 2: An appropriate, general intercessory prayer may be offered by the leader.

Option 3: Prayers may be offered according to local liturgies and customs.

Sharing Our Unity and God's Presence (Communion; sit)

Note: Explanations concerning local distribution procedures and policies may be given.

Option 1: An appropriate Eucharistic liturgy may begin.

Option 2: The following celebration composed of hymns, consecration, distribution, and thanksgiving may be used:

HYMN (of Praise)
Holy God, We Praise Your Name
O Savior, Precious Savior
Lord Jesus Christ, We Humbly Pray

WORDS OF INSTITUTION (Matthew 26:17-19, 26-28)

THE LORD'S PRAYER

THE DISTRIBUTION

HYMNS (during Distribution)
Savior When in Dust to You
Just As I Am
I Lay My Sins on Jesus

Chief of Sinners Though I Be
What a Friend We Have in Jesus

THE PRAYER

L: O Lord, your compassion knows no limits. Continue your love to your people and help us to be transformed through the power of Jesus' cross.

C: Amen.

HYMN (of Thanksgiving)

O Living Bread From Heaven
Now Thank We All Our God
For the Beauty of the Earth

PRAYERS

L: Almighty God, you have made us members of the new covenant community through the gift of your son, Jesus Christ, our Lord. Receive our heart-felt thanksgiving for so great a privilege, and empower us to fulfill our responsibilities as members of your community.

C: Amen.

L: Almighty God, you have given us a vision of new life in the love of your son, Jesus Christ, our Lord. Make us your new creation so that your power will be in us to fulfill that vision of a new world.

C: Amen.

L: Almighty God, you have promised to hear all who come to you. Bless us all, young and old, fat and thin, troubled and at peace, that our church might grow in quality and quantity as we witness to your Word among us.

C: Amen.

Sharing Our Fellowship and God's Peace

Option 1: A community greeting is exchanged.

L: We have gathered as God's people.

C: We have received God's power.

L: We will scatter to live with Christ's love in our daily lives.

C: We will live as God's new creation; we will be God's new covenant community where we live, work, and play.

10

L: We go in peace to serve our Lord.
C: *We go in peace to serve our Lord.*
Option 2: People greet one another as they move about the room with these words: "The love of Christ be with you."

Sharing Our Joy and God's Promise

BENEDICTION (stand) (Romans 12:9-12; 15:5-6; 15:13)
L: Let love be genuine; hate what is evil, hold fast to what is good; love one another with brotherly affection; outdo one another in showing honor. Never flag in zeal, be aglow with the Spirit, serve the Lord.
C: *Rejoice in your hope, be patient in tribulation, be constant in prayer.*
L: May the God of steadfastness and encouragement grant you to live in such harmony with one another, in accord with Christ Jesus, that together you may with one voice glorify the God and Father of our Lord Jesus Christ.
C: *May the God of hope fill you with all joy and peace in believing, so that by the power of the Holy Spirit you may abound in hope. Amen.*

HYMN
Suggested hymns include;
Glories of Your Name Are Spoken
Holy God We Praise Your Name
Built on a Rock
O Love, That Will Not Let Me Go
O Master, Let Me Walk

Good Friday

Christ's Power for New Covenant Compassion

Background

The "Good" in Good Friday reminds us that our worship still contains a note of triumph, even as we reflect on the tremendous cost of our salvation for God's Son. While the mood of our service might be naturally "restrained," we also *already know* the power of the cross to transform even the darkest and most helpless corners of our lives. It is in this context that the individual Christian, as well as our whole community of believers, finds *Christ's Power for New Covenant Compassion* on the Good Friday cross of Jesus Christ.

Setting

1. This service could be a traditional sanctuary service with or without Holy Communion (the Maundy Thursday Communion portion, if not previously used, could be adapted to Good Friday as we consider the new love we have received in Christ).

2. This service could be conducted in a plain room with only folding chairs sitting around the room. This mood might recapture the setting of the disciples as they waited through the time of Jesus' death before Easter. Even a room adjacent to a "public place" with the noise of the world's "business-as-usual" as background could be used (or a recording of such noises could be presented as background during the service).

Symbols

1. All symbols used this night should support the image of the cross and Christ's sacrifice on the cross for our salvation. *The Cross itself* can be highlighted with a draped

cloth, special lighting, special positioning, etc.

2. Nails might be distributed to the congregation at an appropriate time (entrance, sermon, offering, etc.), taking care to place the nails on hands that are opened (rather than hands that are reaching or grasping).*

3. The sound of pounding of nails into wood might be played during an appropriate time of meditation (such as following a Scripture reading, prelude, or postlude time), perhaps interspersed with the "noises" of a crowd (giving imagination time to recreate the original Good Friday scene).

*Note: Like the towel on Maundy Thursday, nails are a common symbol in our everyday life: They hold our houses together; they help us create new things; they support our pictures; and the like. Nails are made of materials of the earth which people here have used in this way to violate God's purposes.

Congregational Introduction of the Good Friday Service
(for written or oral presentation prior to service beginning)

"THE NEW COVENANT'S POWER" is our focus this Holy Week and Easter as we hear once again the Good News (Gospel) for our life together in Jesus Christ. On Good Friday, we personally reflect and meditate on the meaning of the cross, as we remember that *Our Lord's New Covenant Power Creates A New Compassion!* As we recall Jesus' own costly personal sacrifice for our salvation, we experience anew the power of his own transforming love for us as we live and move in the community of God's own people.

(A statement of local beliefs and/or practices concerning Holy Communion or other procedures may follow.)

THE GOOD FRIDAY SERVICE

The New Covenant's Power:
Christ's Power for New Compassion

(Note: It is suggested this service begin with the Invocation instead of the usual Prelude and Hymn. If a hymn should be necessary, one of those following the Invocation may be used to open the service as well. The offering may be received as people enter or leave the sanctuary to keep attention focused on Christ's compassion instead of our response.)

The Power of His Compassion for Faithful Worship

THE INVOCATION (stand; L-Leader; C-Congregation)
L: "Give thanks to the Lord, for he is good;
C: For his steadfast love endures forever."
L: "God shows his love for us in that while we were yet sinners, Christ died for us,"
C: For his steadfast love endures forever.
L: "For if we have been united with him in a death like his, we shall certainly be united with him in a resurrection like his,"
C: For his steadfast love endures forever.
L: "For the wages of sin is death, but the free gift of God is eternal life in Christ Jesus,"
C: For his steadfast love endures forever.
L: "For sin will have no dominion over you, since you are not under law but under grace,"
C: For his steadfast love endures forever.
L: "For I am sure that neither death nor life, nor angels, nor principalities, nor things to come, nor powers, nor height, nor depth, nor anything else in all creation, will be able to separate us from the love of God in Christ Jesus our Lord,"
C: For his steadfast love endures forever.
L: "Give thanks to the Lord, for he is good,
C: For his steadfast love endures forever."
L: (A Prayer of the Day or Collect)
C: Amen.
(Scripture references above are from Psalm 118:1; Romans 6:5; 6:14; 6:23; Romans 8:38-39)

THE HYMN (stand or sit)
Savior, When in Dust to You
Jesus, I Will Ponder Now
Come to Calvary's Holy Mountain
What Wondrous Love Is This
Rock of Ages

The Power of His Compassion for the Way of the Cross (sit)

14

THE FIRST LESSON: Isaiah 53:1-11
    Option 1: Leader reads.
    Option 2: Read responsively as follows:
L: Who has believed what we have heard?
C: *And to whom has the arm of the Lord been revealed?*
L: For he grew up before him like a young plant,
C: *And like a root out of dry ground;*
L: He had no form or comeliness that we should look at him,
C: *And no beauty that we should desire him.*
L: He was despised and rejected by men;
C: *A man of sorrows, and acquainted with grief;*
L: And as one from whom men hide their faces
C: *He was despised, and we esteemed him not.*
L: Surely he has borne our griefs and carried our sorrows;
C: *Yet we esteemed him stricken, smitten by God and afflicted.*
L: But he was wounded for our transgressions,
C: *He was bruised for our iniquities;*
L: Upon him was the chastisement that made us whole,
C: *And with his stripes we are healed.*
L: All we like sheep have gone astray;
C: *We have turned every one to his own way;*
L: And the Lord has laid on him the iniquity of us all.
C: *He was oppressed, and he was afflicted, yet he opened not his mouth;*
L: Like a lamb that is led to the slaughter,
C: *And like a sheep that before its shearers is dumb, so he opened not his mouth.*
L: By oppression and judgment he was taken away;
C: *And as for his generation, who considered that he was cut off out of the land of the living, stricken for the transgression of my people?*
L: And they made his grave with the wicked
C: *And with a rich man in his death,*
L: Although he had done no violence,
C: *And there was no deceit in his mouth.*
L: Yet it was the will of the Lord to bruise him;
C: *He has put him to grief;*
L: When he makes himself an offering for sin,
C: *He shall see his offspring, he shall prolong his days;*
L: The will of the Lord shall prosper in his hands;
C: *He shall see the fruit of the travail of his soul and be satisfied;*

L: By his knowledge shall the righteous one, my servant, make many to be accounted righteous;
C: *And he shall bear their iniquities.*

SILENCE FOR MEDITATION (Approximately 2 minutes)

THE HYMN and/or ANTHEM
An anthem should reflect either the concept of old covenant "fulfillment" or the "suffering servant" on the Cross.
Hymn suggestions include;
Ah, Holy Jesus
In the Cross of Christ I Glory
Beneath the Cross of Jesus
My Hope Is Built on Nothing Less
Beautiful Savior

THE SECOND LESSON: 1 Corinthians 1:18-2:5

SILENCE FOR MEDITATION (approximately 2 minutes)

THE HYMN and/or ANTHEM
An anthem should reflect the concept of "salvation" or the image of the Cross itself.
Hymn suggestions include;
In the Cross of Christ I Glory
Beneath the Cross of Jesus
O Sacred Head Now Wounded
Wide Open Are Your Hands
The Old Rugged Cross

THE GOSPEL LESSON
Option 1. John 19:17-30
Option 2: John 18:1-19:42, a dramatic reading as the sermon

SILENCE FOR MEDITATION (approximately 2 minutes)

THE HYMN
Amazing Grace

THE PROCLAMATION
Option 1: A traditional message on the tremendous love which has brought us our salvation. (John 3:16,17)

Option 2: A message on the gift of Christ who empowers us to live with him and his compassion in the midst of the same world of: (1) Criticism, (2) Loneliness, (3) Selfishness, (4) Injustice, (5) Suffering and Death.

Option 3: A prepared dramatic reading of John 18: 1-19:42 at the time of the Gospel reading above, instead of here.

SILENCE FOR MEDITATION

The Power of His Compassion for Human Need

Living in his Love (stand or kneel) (based on 1 Corinthians 13)

L: Our Lord chose the way of love, which is patient and kind.

C: *Thank you, Lord Jesus, for being so patient and kind toward us when we are so sinful and short-sighted. Increase our patience and kindness toward those who touch our lives, that we might live faithful to your covenant.*

L: Our Lord chose the way of love, which is not jealous or boastful.

C: *Thank you, Lord Jesus, for choosing the way of the cross and including us in your plan of salvation while we were yet sinful. Help us to be just as inclusive of all people and preserve us from being possessive or proud in ways that deny your cross.*

L: Our Lord chose the way of love which is not arrogant or rude.

C: *Thank you, Lord Jesus, for continuing to be with us in such an affirming way, even though we have done nothing to deserve it. Empower us, your people, to continually reject the ways of our world when they would make us arrogant or rude.*

L: Our Lord chose the way of love, which does not insist on its own way and is not irritable or resentful.

C: *Thank you, Lord Jesus, for giving us the freedom to choose to follow your way even though we are often still not faithful to it. Cleanse us from those things which make us irritable and resentful toward others, that we may never begrudge your choice which leads to our life eternal.*

L: Our Lord chose the way of love, which does not

rejoice at wrong, but rejoices in the right.

C: *Thank you, Lord Jesus, for forgiving us at so great a personal cost. As we live in your forgiveness, we rejoice that you have made us fit for your Kingdom. Help us to pass on the Word of compassion and forgiveness in our attitudes and actions, that all people might rejoice with us.*

L: Our Lord chose the way of love, which bears all things, believes all things, hopes all things, endures all things, and is the greatest choice of all possible ways.

C: *Thank you, Lord Jesus, for showing us the greatest way of all through your suffering love as revealed in the events of this Holy Week. Bless us as we praise your name and look to you to fill our hunger for righteousness.*

L: (Other petitions or prayers may be received from the congregation with an appropriate response.)

C: *Amen.*

SILENCE (for personal acceptance and affirmation of his way of new love)

Living by His Values

Option 1: Traditional Lord's Prayer

Option 2: Lord's Prayer Litany

L: Our Father who art in heaven,

C: *As children of God, we value his love for us more than anything else. We want the compassion of his Son Jesus Christ to live in us and through us.*

L: Hallowed be thy name,

C: *As a people made holy in Christ, we value God's name. We use Jesus' name in our daily lives as we seek the love necessary to live by the priorities of our Lord.*

L: Thy Kingdom come,

C: *As inheritors of the Kingdom of Christ, we value our new community. We desire to be loving workers and faithful citizens of Christ's way, truth, and life.*

L: Thy will be done, on earth as it is in heaven,

C: *As stewards of the mysteries of God, we value the standards of living taught by Jesus Christ. We desire faith, hope, and love more than we desire the treasures of our world.*

18

L: Give us this day our daily bread,
C: *As creatures of the earth, we value the things God uses to care for our physical needs. We treasure our relationship to all of creation and lovingly seek to care for the natural environment of God's providence.*
L: And forgive us our trespasses,
C: *As people baptized into the death and resurrection of Christ, we value the love of Jesus made visible on the cross. We turn to face God with the confidence which comes only from Christ's forgiveness on the cross.*
L: As we forgive those who trespass against us,
C: *As forgiven disciples of Christ, we value forgiveness as a way of life. We seek to live by a lifestyle that forgives our families, our friends, and even our enemies.*
L: And lead us not into temptation,
C: *As Jesus' followers, we value our faith which redirects our vision when we are tempted. We walk, keeping our focus on the compassionate Savior in order to keep away from as much temptation as possible.*
L: But deliver us from evil,
C: *As pilgrims on earth for a brief time, we value our Lord's salvation which secures our home in heaven. We work now for the glory of Christ and his love which frees us all from injustice, oppression, and other evils.*
L: For thine is the kingdom and the power and the glory forever and ever.
C: *Amen.*

HYMN (or Communion may begin here — see page 8)
Praise God From Whom All Blessings Flow (Doxology)

Living With His Blessing (stand)

BENEDICTION
Option 1: A local or traditional blessing.
Option 2: "May you be strengthened with all power, according to his glorious might, for all endurance and patience with joy, giving thanks to the Father, who has qualified us to share in the inheritance of the saints in light. He has delivered us from the dominion of darkness

and transferred us to the kingdom of his beloved Son, in whom we have redemption, the forgiveness of sins." (Colossians 1:11-14)

THE HYMN
Were You There
Christ, the Life of All the Living
O Sacred Head, Now Wounded
My Faith Looks up to Thee
Lord Dismiss Us With Your Blessing

Easter Sunrise

Christ's Power for New Covenant Celebration

Background

Easter is the oldest celebration of the Christian Church. Since the earliest days, Christians have gathered on the first day of the week *to celebrate* Christ's life, death, and resurrection. Since Easter is a part of every Sunday, Easter Sunday itself could be likened to an unrestrained, gala, surprise party of happiness. Therefore, Easter Day worship unfolds an experience of *Christ's Power for New Covenant Celebration.*

Setting

1. This sunrise service could be in an outdoor setting, in a regular sanctuary setting, or in a home.
2. This sunrise service includes a Holy Communion portion which could be omitted (as in the case of some ecumenical settings).
3. This service could be included as part of an early *pot-luck* congregational breakfast.

Symbols

1. In a service of great celebration and victory, music and its instruments can be a most effective symbol. Special string, brass, and percussion instruments for accompaniment can stimulate increased celebration. Beginning (Prelude) with string, adding brass (Opening Hymn) and swelling to include percussion by the Closing Hymn would be ideal.
2. Special banners with bright, colorful motifs, utilizing the empty cross, the butterfly, the lily, sunlight, as well as modern designs, will aid in the celebration.
3. Individual, hand-crafted name tags with a symbol (see

No. 2 above) could be given each person upon entering. A small plant, grown from a seed (not a cut flower) could also be given to capture the "new creation" coming from the "death" of the seed. (see 1 Corinthians 15)

    4. Marching in procession and/or recession creates a festive mood. All children could march while singing a prepared song; a choir could sing while marching; etc.

    5. The main symbol on Easter is the person of the Risen Christ. He, not gardens or tombs, is the New Covenant.

Congregational Introduction of the Easter Sunrise Service
(for written or oral presentation prior to service beginning)

    "THE NEW COVENANT'S POWER" is our focus this Easter in worship as we hear the Good News of our Lord's victory over the Cross. On Easter, we join in rejoicing over the new life we share in Jesus Christ. We come together again today so that we might experience that *Our Lord's New Covenant Power Creates a New Celebration!* As we see our Risen Lord ready to greet us with faith and hope that is positive, powerful, and permanent, we respond with resounding praise.

    (If offered, a statement of local beliefs and/or procedures concerning Holy Communion may follow.)

THE EASTER SUNRISE SERVICE

The New Covenant's Power:
Christ's Power for New Celebration

We Celebrate the Purpose of His Life

THE PRELUDE (such as "Morning Has Broken")

THE GOOD NEWS ANNOUNCEMENT: Matthew 28:1-10 (sit)
    Option 1: This announcement could be read from the rear of the assembly.
    Option 2: This reading could be taped on a morning newspaper, giving the appearance of sharing news, and read from one side of the front of the assembly.

THE PROCESSIONAL HYMN (stand)
    Suggested hymns include:

22

Jesus Christ Is Risen Today
Lift High the Cross
Praise to the Lord, the Almighty
Crown Him With Many Crowns
A Hymn of Glory Let Us Sing

THE INVOCATION (L-Leader; A-Assisting person(s) in assembly; C-Congregation)
L: Let the celebration begin!
A: We celebrate Jesus Christ, "a man of sorrows, and acquainted with grief."
C: *We will greatly rejoice in the Lord.*
A: We celebrate Jesus Christ, who "bore the sin of many, and made intercession for the transgressors."
C: We will greatly rejoice in the Lord.
A: We celebrate Jesus Christ, sent "to bring good tidings to the afflicted . . . to bind up the broken-hearted . . . to proclaim liberty to the captives . . . to comfort all who mourn."
C: *We will greatly rejoice in the Lord.*
A: We celebrate Jesus Christ, who "humbled himself and became obedient unto death, even death on a cross."
C: *We will greatly rejoice in the Lord.*
A: We celebrate Jesus Christ, who taught us to seek God's kingdom first; who taught us to love our enemies; who taught us to have trust in God; who taught us how to truly love one another.
C: *We will greatly rejoice in the Lord.*
A: We celebrate Jesus Christ, who healed many diseases, who withstood many temptations, who cast out many demons, who called many people to discipleship, who gave us all the Holy Spirit.
C: *We will greatly rejoice in the Lord.*
A: We celebrate Jesus Christ, who brought us salvation, forgiveness, freedom, fellowship, faith, hope, and love.
C: *We will greatly rejoice in the Lord.*
L: We celebrate Jesus Christ, who changes us and our daily lives forever and ever.
C: *(The Prayer of the Day or Easter Collect)*

(Scripture references quoted above include Isaiah 53:3; 53:12; 61:1-2; Philippians 2:8)

THE HYMN (sit)
Suggested hymns include;
I Know My Redeemer Lives
Keep in Mind That Jesus Christ Has Died for Us
O Worship the King
Now All the Vault of Heaven Resounds
All Hail the Power of Jesus' Name

We Celebrate the Promise of His Life

MORE GOOD NEWS: John 14:1-14 (sit)
(Note: This reading should be done in the same manner
as the first Good News announcement.)

DRAMATIC DIALOGUE
(Assumes three readers or participants who can simply
arise from where they are seated.)
Person 1: No one keeps promises anymore. Promises
are a dime a dozen!
Person 2: Parents, kids, salesmen, advertisers,
politicians — everyone makes promises. If
someone can get ahead or make an extra
buck with a promise, they'll do it for sure!
Person 1: Sure! How can we believe Jesus? Wasn't he
just trying to get a following? After all, don't
we have greater power today than he did?
And who gets everything they ask for?
Person 3: We find it hard to believe promises and trust
others in a world where words and talk are
cheap. Only when we get to know someone
personally, do we discover if they are
dependable.
Person 2: Are you suggesting we have to take a chance
before we can know if Jesus keeps his
promises?
Person 3: Yes and no! We can talk with people who
know him and have claimed his promises.
Yet we can only know for sure when we personally risk our lives by following him and
his ways.
Person 1: I know some people who keep their promises. But not very many.

24

Person 2: It would be refreshing to know someone who really keeps **all** his promises.

Person 3: And that's the secret — we can only choose to receive all of Jesus' promises. Too many people just want to pick and choose what they want for their own benefit.

Person 2: You mean we can't negotiate with Jesus to change the agreement he has offered us? We can only decide yes or no to his **whole package?**

Person 1: No wonder I haven't gotten what I asked for in the past — I was trying to change Jesus' agreement, instead of letting him change me.

Person 3: Now we got it! It's all or nothing with Jesus. We have to take the whole covenant with both our cross *and* crown.

Person 1: Well, what are the promises of Jesus?

LITANY OF PROMISES

L: When we believe in Jesus, we will find our salvation.

C: *"He who believes and is baptized will be saved; but he who does not believe will be condemned."*

L: When we abide in Jesus now, we will live with him forever.

C: *"When I go and prepare a place for you, I will come again and will take you to myself, that where I am you may be also."*

L: When we give Jesus our top priority in our daily living, he will care for our daily needs.

C: *"Seek first his kingdom and his righteousness, and all these things shall be yours as well."*

L: When we desire and ask for success in living by God's standards and values, he will give us the power we need to deny ourselves and follow him.

C: *"Ask and it will be given you; seek, and you will find; knock, and it will be opened to you."*

L: When we live in the new covenant Christ our daily lives will change for the better.

C: *"I am the vine, you are the branches. He who abides in me, and I in him, he it is that bears much fruit, for apart from me you can do nothing."*

L: When we need guidance and power, Jesus will bless us through the Holy Spirit.

C: "And I will pray to the Father, and he will give you another Counselor, to be with you forever." (John 14:16)

L: When our faith results in faithful actions and moral living, we will find personal stability.

C: "Not everyone who says to me, 'Lord, Lord,' shall enter the kingdom of heaven, but he who does the will of my Father who is in heaven . . . everyone then who hears these words of mine and does them will be like a wise man who built his house upon the rock . . ." (Matthew 7:21, 24)

(Scripture references above include: Mark 16:16; John 14:3; Matthew 6:33; Matthew 7:7; John 15:5; John 14:16; Matthew 7:21, 24)

SPECIAL MUSIC

Option 1: An instrumental solo for personal reflection time.

Option 2: Any combination of voices and/or instruments causing reflection on Jesus' promises to his disciples.

HYMN

Suggested hymns include:
God of Grace and God of Glory
Earth and All Stars!
A Mighty Fortress Is Our God
A Hymn of Glory Let Us Sing
All Hail the Power of Jesus Name

MEDITATION

Option 1: A sermon based on Colossians 3:1-4 or Romans 6:5.

Option 2: A Scripture reading such as John 20:11-23 or 1 Corinthians 15:1-58.

Option 3: A dramatic presentation.

Option 4: A silent time of personal reflection on a pre-printed theme or text.

Option 5: Omit and continue with the service.

We Celebrate the Presence of His Life

THE HYMN

Suggested hymns include:

26

Christ Is Risen! Alleluia!
He Is Arisen! Glorious Word!
Ye Watchers and Ye Holy Ones
Let All Things Now Living
Now We Join in Celebration (Communion)

THE OFFERING
Offertory Response (as gifts are returned)
Praise God From Whom All Blessings Flow (Doxology)

THE PRAYERS
L: Almighty Lord, we confess our need for your loving forgiveness.
C: *We have violated our created purpose by failing to love you with our whole heart. We have tried to renegoiate your gracious covenant, to make it more compromising with the ways of our world.*
L: We confess our need for new love.
C: *We have made a mess of things by failing to love one another as you have loved us. Our commitment to your way is less than total in our relationships with our friends and enemies.*
L: We confess our need for new faith.
C: *We have forsaken our beliefs and convictions too quickly for the sake of momentary pleasures and conveniences. Our faith is fickle and changes on demand.*
L: We confess our need for new hope.
C: *We have forgotten the vision of eternal life and heavenly purposes which our Lord Jesus gave us for our daily living. Our lives are depressed and we have lost our zeal by focusing on the day's own problems instead of Christ Jesus.*
L: We confess our need for new joy.
C: *We have lost our joy in eternal values too frequently. Our spirits are quick to return to the ways of the world where we wallow without a sense of permanent victory.*
L: We confess our need for new peace.
C: *We have gained only restless hearts from our failure to find assurance and confidence by our own efforts. Our hearts find only turmoil and war apart from our trust in your loving care.*
L: We confess our need for new justice.

C: *We have accepted injustice as inevitable and unchangeable. Our eyes are no longer shocked or incensed when we see innocent suffering and death.*

L: We confess our need for new priorities.

C: *We have neglected to seek* **first** *our Lord's kingdom. Our minds are content to seek your ways as our second or third priorities.*

L: We confess our need for new creation.

C: *We have given our old sinful self too much authority. Our resolves, resolutions, and intentions are too weak to get the job done without your Spirit.*

L: We confess our need for new changes.

C: *We have spoiled the earth with our greed. Our carelessness has resulted in the pollution of nature, the passion of violence, and the perversion of your plan for our world.*

L: Even before we have confessed our needs, God has provided us a life of community, compassion, and celebration in our Lord Jesus Christ. in his victory we have received the free gift of new life. In his love, we have received the free gift of salvation. In his determination and commitment to us, we have received the free gift of God's own leadership.

C: *We accept God's new life for us! We rejoice in our Lord's victory! We celebrate our Lord's love! We praise him for his leadership!*

L: Let us pray that God will bring others to hear the same Good News of God's New Covenant power in Christ Jesus.

C: *O Lord, grant that all people might have the opportunity to hear the Gospel of our Lord Jesus Christ.*

L: Let us pray that God will cause our own Church community to grow, in quality and quantity, that more people might be converted to Christ and discover fresh opportunities for serving in his name.

C: *O Lord, give our Church the growth in grace that will benefit all people in your world.*

L: Let us pray that God will use us, through our daily lives, our resources, and our prayers, to bring others to faith in Jesus Christ.

C: *O Lord, move us to seek those people who will accept our witness and your Word.*

L: Let us pray that God will bless all who suffer afflictions of body, mind, or spirit, (especially remembering

28

      _____,) and others according to
their special needs.

C: *O Lord, heal people in need of your special care and use us to express your love to them.*

L: Let us pray that God will unite his people in one Christian (or catholic) Church, that all people might know the power of his name.

C: *O Lord, heal all wounds that divide your body and cause us hurt.*

L: Let us pray that God will gather the hopes and dreams of all his people and make us good stewards of his purposes.

C: *O Lord, bless us with your continued Lordship over our lives, over our world, and over all creation.*

L: Let us unite our hearts and minds, as we embrace the values of his kingdom while we pray our Lord's Prayer,

C: *(The Lord's Prayer)*

THE PEACE (People greet one another with a personal word of blessing.)

THE HYMN (sit)
If there is no Communion:
Earth and All Stars!
Battle Hymn of the Republic
Crown Him With Many Crowns
If there is Communion:
Come Let Us Eat
Now We Join in Celebration
Let Us Break Bread Together

THE COMMUNION (stand)

Thanksgiving (Philippians 4:4-7)
L: Rejoice in the Lord always;
C: *The Lord is at hand!*
L: Have no anxiety about anything;
C: *The Lord is at hand!*
L: The peace of God, which passes all understanding, will keep your hearts and minds in Christ Jesus.
C: *Alleluia!*

Prayer

L: Almighty God, we join your whole Church in praising you for the glorious resurrection of your Son, Jesus Christ, our Lord; receive our thanksgiving and enable his power to live in us as we come to his Supper.

C: Amen. Come Lord Jesus.

L: (Words of Institution: from 1 Corinthians 11:23-26 or local liturgy)

C: Amen. Come Lord Jesus.

Distribution (sit)

Hymn

Sent Forth by God's Blessing
Praise to the Lord, the Almighty
I Know That My Redeemer Lives!

THE BENEDICTION (stand)

THE HYMN

Thine Is the Glory
On Our Way Rejoicing
Crown Him With Many Crowns
O, Worship the King
Lift High the Cross
Onward Christian Soldiers

POSTLUDE

www.ingramcontent.com/pod-product-compliance
Lightning Source LLC
Chambersburg PA
CBHW060044040426
42331CB00032B/2373